CW00927144

The Roof-Climber's Guide to
ST JOHN'S

With a plan and illustrations

By A. Climber

OLEANDER PRESS

The Oleander Press
16 Orchard Street
Cambridge
CB1 1JT

www.oleanderpress.com

First published by Metcalfe & Co Ltd, Trinity Street: 1921
This edition published by The Oleander Press: 2009

A CIP catalogue record for the book is
available from the British Library.

ISBN: 9780906672952

Designed and typeset by Hamish Symington
www.hamishsymington.com

Printed in England

Contents

To the author of *The Roof-Climber's Guide to Trinity*

Preface

It is with some trepidation that we venture to lay this little book before the public, for it has been so hastily put together from the minute-books of the Club, that the style can in no way do justice to the subject-matter, and the book must inevitably fall far short of its delightful little fore-runner, the *Roof-Climber's Guide to Trinity*.

To the author of the Trinity Guide we owe so many hours of glorious folly on the roofs, that we are glad to have this opportunity of showing him our gratitude. It was his idealism which turned our moonlight escapades into an honourable sport. From him we learnt the 'spirit' of the game. From him we learnt the motto: *"Though there's doorway behind thee and window before, go straight at the wall"*.

If this little book could only inspire others to follow in his footsteps, then its object is accomplished.

For purposes of description we have followed the conventional method of dividing the College into Routes. It must not, however, be assumed that the route is necessarily to be completed in one attempt. The description given is by no means exhaustive, for each ridge and traverse can be tackled in endless different ways.

Elucidation of Plan

A	Reading Room Turret	M	Dean's Highway
B	Main Gate Tower	N	Shrewsbury Tower
C	Bicycle Shed Ridge	O	South Ridge
D	Ivy Arch	P	Broad Chimney Stack
E	Essex Ridge	R	Kitchen Turret
F	Hall Ridge	S	Library Plateau
G	Bell Pinnacle	T	Furnace Hole
H	Eagle Pinnacle	U	Great Pinnacle
J	Gunning's Turret	V	Corner Towers
K	Chapel Tower	W	Chapel Court Col
L	Ghost Walk	X	Chapel Court Pinnacle

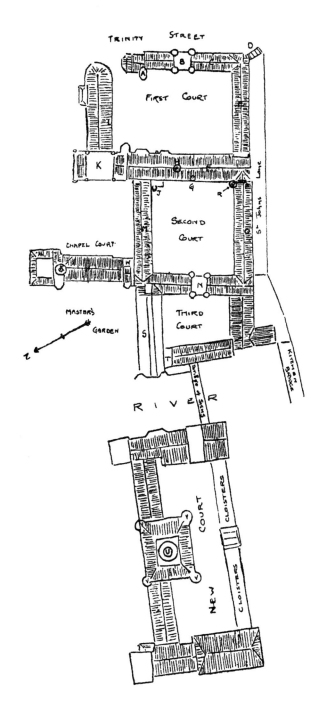

TRINITY STREET

FIRST COURT

K

Chapel Court

SECOND COURT

St Johns Lane

MASTER'S GARDEN

THIRD COURT

RIVER

KITCHEN BRIDGE

BRIDGE OF SIGHS

NEW COURT

CLOISTERS

CLOISTERS

Route A: First Court

The complete circuit of First Court is unfortunately impossible owing to the gap between the East End of the Chapel and the Reading Room Building, but the roofs can be followed as far as they go.

Reading Room Turret: We will imagine that the start of our route is made from some attic window between the Main Gate Tower and Reading Room Turret. Before the real business of the evening begins, and if time permits, a pleasant little scramble can be found among the Reading Room Ridges. The climber is amply repaid for his trouble by the view that he gains of St John's

Street. The Turret itself can be climbed without much difficulty by the 'human ladder' method[1]; but its battlements require very careful handling and should on no account be trusted. They are, in fact, the loosest that we have come across in the College, and the slightest pressure, which is not vertically applied, would send them crashing into the roof below.

Main Gate Tower: Retracing our steps for a short distance, we arrive at the foot of Main Gate Tower – our first serious proposition. It rises some twenty feet above the gutter in which we are standing, and has two drain-pipes running up its north face – one on the St John's Street side of Reading Room Ridge, the other on the First Court side. The former stops short just below the battlements, whereas the latter runs up

---

1   By the "human ladder" method it is possible to surmount a blank wall thirteen feet in height. Sometimes a fifteen-foot wall can be climbed in the same way, if there is a good hand-hold half-way up. The procedure is as follows: The leader mounts on the back of the second man, who slowly straightens himself up to his full height. (Both are facing the wall.) By this time the leader will probably be able to reach the top of the wall and pull himself up. If, however, he is still not high enough, he must find some grip for the hands (a ledge or hole in the wall) and take his weight off the shoulders of the man below. The latter is then able to substitute hands for shoulders, and push the leader still further up to the full extent of the arms.

above them and so facilitates the climb. We therefore choose this pipe and begin the ascent from the gutter on the First Court side of the roof. For the first seven feet the pipe is too close into the wall to allow for a good hand-hold, but afterwards there is a stretch of about four feet, when the pipe is well clear of the wall. It is followed by another stretch, where the pipe gets too close for any grip at all. This is the difficult part of the climb. A short search, however, will disclose a small hole in the wall, where a brick has worn away. This is to the left and about as high as the foot can be raised. The foot-hold is precarious, but it enables a long stretch of the arm to be made up to the point where the pipe bends round a sloping ledge. Here the pipe is well clear of the wall and a good grip can be obtained. A short scramble enables one to stand on the sloping wall, and the remainder of the climb presents no difficulty.

The crux of the whole climb is the hole in the brick half-way up the pipe. If it is not found, a man who is strong in the wrists can scramble up to security, but only with the strength born of despair. There is a nasty sky-light at the foot of the tower, through which one might fall, if an accident occurred.

The four corner turrets on the top of the Tower could be tackled by the human-ladder method, but on the only occasion on which the Main Gate has been ascended, we were pressed for time and so passed them by.

For purposes of descent onto the Bicycle Shed roof there is again a choice of two pipes, one at each corner of the Tower. Neither pipe runs up as far as the battlements, so in either case it is necessary to lower oneself onto the bowl of the pipe and then transfer the hands to the level of the feet. In the case of the pipe on the First Court side of the Tower, this gymnastic feat is made quite easy by a narrow gap between the battlements and the projecting corner-turret. As one bends down to bring the hands to the level of the feet, the left shoulder can be pressed against the turret, and the possibility of a fall is almost obviated. The descent of the pipe itself presents no difficulty until about seven feet from the ground, when it gets very close into the wall and it becomes necessary to put both hands round the same side of the pipe, in order to grip at all. The descent can then be continued by bringing the hands down to the level of the feet and, so to speak, walking down the wall.

Taken as a whole the Main Gate offers one of the most interesting and difficult climbs in the College – one which compares favourably with the Trinity Great Gate itself. The latter, by reason of its great height, imposes a far more serious strain upon the muscles, but the climbing is perfectly straightforward and calls for no resource and finesse, as does the Main Gate of St Johns. The one is purely a question of strength, the other of skill.

The whole climb takes a party of three about twenty minutes to half an hour to accomplish. The party should be roped.

Ivy Arch: Moving rapidly along Bicycle Shed Ridge, we come to the interesting little corner from which it is possible to gain the roofs of Trinity without descending to the ground. The bridge (known as Ivy Arch), which connects the two Colleges, is dealt with later.

The Hall: The Essex building presents no difficulty, and we soon arrive at the foot of Hall Ridge. We now have three alternatives before us: (1) To walk along the balcony on the First Court side of the Ridge; (2) To take the high level route along the Ridge itself; (3) To cross the Ridge and work our way along the Second Court side. The first alternative is far and away the simplest and quickest. The second or high-level route is badly porter-swept, and on one occasion the party was discovered silhouetted clearly against the sky-line. The porters ran out into the Court and a chase ensued. So the whole party took to their hands and heels and careered like so many monkeys over the slates into safety. The roof of the Hall is very steep and it is best climbed by the human-ladder method. Having arrived on the Ridge we move along it in the direction of the Chapel and find our progress barred by four obstacles; a small kitchen ventilator (easily surmounted), two chimney-stacks, and the lantern on the Hall, known as Eagle Pinnacle. The first of the stacks can be turned by walking round the ledge at the foot of the chimneys. But the ledge on the second stack is very crumbly, and it is wiser to yield to caution and step down the roof, embracing the stack with both hands, until it is possible to swing round and up again. Eagle Pinnacle can easily be turned, but an ascent to its summit has not yet been accomplished. A solitary climber once attempted it, but found it too dangerous without assistance. It is made entirely of wood, lead, and glass. The ornamental ribs are for the most part rotten, and the wooden spire at the top is badly split. A man standing on the Hall Ridge can just reach the over-hanging cornice and pull himself up by the arms. But the cornice (of lead) begins to bend and the wooden foot-holes start to crack. If a second man were sitting on the ridge below, assistance from him might just make it possible for the climb to be accomplished. The climb may be attempted either from the Chapel side or the Trinity side of the Pinnacle. On the Chapel side the window has projecting hinges which give good support to the feet, but the wood-work is more rotten than on the other side. On the Trinity side the wood-work is moderately secure (by comparison!). There are no hinges to the window and the foot-holes are not so good, but there is a very strong lightning-conductor running up on the left of the window. On the whole the climb is probably safer on this side than on the Chapel side.

The third and last alternative route, namely, to cross Hall Ridge and work along its Second Court side, belongs properly to the circuit of Second Court. There is a series of gables to be crossed. But, after disposing of the first three, one is surprised to find that the remaining four are false gables and have a passage-way cut through them. The laborious process of clambering over each one is, therefore, rendered superfluous. Immediately above the centre gable stands Bell Pinnacle, which at once attracts our attention. It is not difficult to climb to its summit. The two long iron stays, which secure it to the roof, are absolutely firm and quite invaluable during the first part of the climb. After passing through the last of the false gables we come to Gunning's Balcony, a flat, leaden platform, which projects into Second Court. Here, if the moonlight be strong enough, it is possible to decipher a most interesting little inscription, carved with a pen-knife in the lead:–

PETRUS
GUNNING
ELIENSIS
HUJUS COLL : ALUMNUS
FEB: 19TH
1734

This is the earliest record that we have of the Alpine Club!

The Chapel: Having traversed the whole length of the Hall Ridge by one of the three routes above described, it is a simple matter to clamber onto the balcony which runs round the Chapel. This balcony, which goes by the name of Ghost Walk, is lined throughout with 'duck-boards', and is only just broad enough to walk along. Squeezing our way through, however, we reach the east end of the Chapel with its quaint view of St John's

Street. Pushing on round the far side, we are on the point of completing the tour of the Chapel, when further progress is stopped by the fact that the walk, which has gradually grown narrower and narrower, comes to an abrupt end. As we retrace our steps, we are certain to make an attempt upon the slate roof of the Chapel. But the steepness of its slope and the smoothness of its surface are almost equally certain to preclude success, unless the unsporting device be adopted of throwing a rope over from one side of the ridge to the other. There are many stories current of the undergraduate who climbed the face of the Chapel Tower in daylight, while the porters waited patiently below. They are all delightful and all completely mythical. Anyone with a knowledge of climbing can see that such a feat is unfortunately impossible.

Route B: Circuit of Second Court

Second Court offers little of interest to the climber; perhaps the only difficulty is that of escaping the vigilance of the porter. It is also advisable to bear in mind that there is a veritable bee-hive of dons to the north and south sides of the Court. Above all things avoid disturbing the Dean!

There are innumerable ways of obtaining access to the roof. In fact, any attempt to 'stop up the holes' would be of little avail. Let us assume that we are somewhere in the neighbourhood of Kitchen Turret.

The Hall roof, which has been dealt with already, only takes five minutes, when we arrive at the commencement of the roof on the north side of the Court, appropriately labelled the 'Dean's Highway'. A 'wayside problem' here presents itself, namely, Gunning's Turret. This is about eighteen feet in height and looks very difficult. It has as yet not been seriously attempted. A pipe runs up one side; for the first six feet it is loose, but it is possible to grip above the joint, where it is firmer, and pull up. But at about ten feet up the pipe gets very close to the wall and further progress is impossible. There is, however, a window some fifteen feet up and to the left of the pipe. It might be possible to reach this by the human-ladder method, and then to swing out to the pipe, in the hope of finding a finger-grip upon it. Unfortunately the window has no upper moulding for the hands to grip.

It is on the whole best to travel along the apex of the roof of the Dean's Highway. Patience and care take us across safely, and the Dean is left behind in blissful ignorance. Turning to the left we traverse the apex of the roof on the east side of the Court and are then faced with the Shrewsbury Tower.

Shrewsbury Tower: A drainpipe will be found running up the tower on the eastward side of the ridge. This is a little loose, but can easily be scaled. A similar pipe will be found on the other side of the tower, which brings us down again to the roof, and the climb is continued as before.

The south roof presents nothing of importance, and we are now back where we started from in the region of Kitchen Turret.

Kitchen Turret: The climber cannot fail to be attracted by this pretty little climb, and it is perhaps the only thing of interest in Route B.

One can reach the top of the turret by means of a somewhat rickety drainpipe which lies against the Trinity side. A small window on the right of the pipe is of considerable assistance.

A better and more venturesome climb can be made by 'back-and-kneeing' between the turret and the broad chimney stack. Starting with one's back towards the turret and one's feet against the stack, with considerable effort the first seven feet can be effected. Once the ledge round the stack is reached things become easier. After about eight feet more one arrives at a ledge on the turret, which can be circumvented by climbing up the left instead of up the centre of the chimney. Once seated upon this ledge it is comparatively easy to finish on the stack.

Route C: Circuit
of Third Court

Only a very short account of Route C is required, as
there is nothing attractive beyond the exquisite view of
the river from the library, which should not be missed.

Commencing on the north side of Shrewsbury Tower
a short climb brings us to the library roof. After visit-
ing the west end of the roof to view the river we leave
the library via the arch shown in the sketch on the
opposite page by means of a narrow ledge (about five
inches broad). The climb is easy, but it is a position in
which a rope should be used. We are now on the west

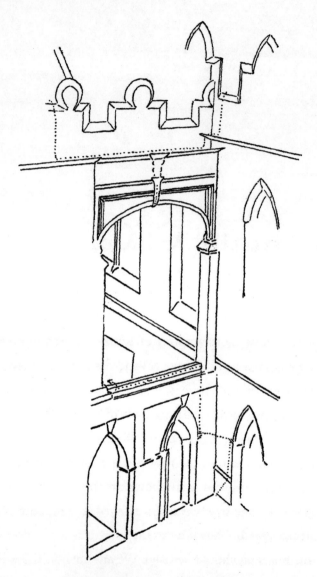

North-West Corner, Third Court.

building which overlooks the river. Progress along the river side of the roof is laborious owing to the chimney stacks. The Third Court side has a balcony along its entire length. A similar balcony on the south side takes us past a Don's rooms (where it is best to keep low) to the western building of Second Court. The circuit is completed by crossing over Shrewsbury Tower in a reverse direction to that layed down in Route B.

Route D:
Chapel Court

Of all the climbs in St John's this is the one which was hardest to work out. The difficulty lay, not so much in the climbing, as in the discovery of the one and only method by which the Chapel Court heights can be reached.

Chapel Court Col: Exploration showed that the most promising line of attack lay over the lower slopes, which form the 'col' between Dean's Highway and the Chapel Court heights themselves. It was therefore decided to

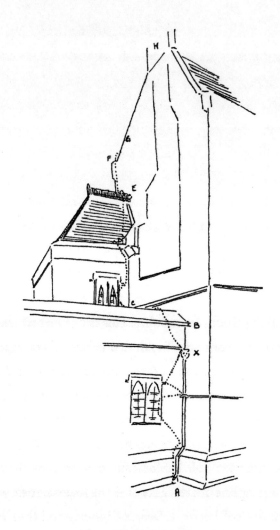

Chapel Court Col.

A to B: 18ft. C to D: 10ft. D to E: 10ft. E to G: 8ft.

make an attempt upon the col. Failure attended the first efforts of a solitary climber, who tried the ascent from the Master's garden side. But a second attempt from the Chapel side (starting from the grass plot immediately under the Dean's study window) met with better success. The climb may be divided in four pitches (see sketch, p. 20).

(1) A to B (about 18 feet). The first part of the pitch is comparatively simple, as the iron bars and mouldings of the window lend considerable assistance during the ascent of the pipe. But at the point where the pipe stops short (marked X in sketch) one is absolutely held up for a time. There is one good foothold on the moulding above the window, and this enables the back to be pressed firmly into the wall of Chapel Court. The other foot is dangling loosely in the air, and the hand-hold on the narrow ledge at the top of the pipe is most insecure. One hand must, however, be taken off and raised until it can grip the balustrade at B. The manoeuvre is an excellent balance test. The descent of this pitch is not nearly so hard.

(2) C to D (about 10 feet). This is quite easy, the window again assisting. The return journey is harder than

it looks, and the last two feet are quite tricky. (One does not like to jump for fear of arousing the Dean).

(3) D to E (about 10 feet). No difficulty.

(4) E to F. This is the most interesting pitch of all. On arrival at the ridge E one is completely held up by a blank wall eight feet high. The first attempt to scale it was a failure, but is perhaps worth describing. Two cushions were placed on the apex of the ridge E, and one man sat astride the roof upon the cushions (the roof is sharp and could not be sat upon firmly without cushions!). The leader, who had been sitting behind him, then stood up on the ridge and stepped on to his shoulders. Very slowly the second man raised his bent back until he was sitting at his full height. By this time the leader (who had been keeping his balance by leaning on his hands against the blank wall) had been raised sufficiently high for him to be able to grip the sloping balustrade of the Chapel Court roof at G. The balustrade was sloping at such an angle, however, that he was unable to pull himself up on to the roof, even though the second man had substituted hands for shoulders. The difficulty lay in the fact that the pull up

had to be done entirely with the left arm, and the more the climber pulled the further the roof swung him out to the left and over space.

The descent from so precarious a position was easier than had been hoped. The sitting man bent slowly forward, and then the leader moved from the standing to the sitting position astride his shoulders. Throughout the manoeuvre the leader had been roped direct to a third man who was anchored at the point D. This would have prevented a really serious fall over the edge of the col into the Master's garden.

Having failed by this method we looked around for a fresh line of attack. The only possible spot appeared to be the left-hand corner of the roof (at the point F). To attempt a human-ladder climb from immediately below it appeared to be madness, partly because of the height (about 18 feet), and partly because of the dangerous fall into the Master's garden, which would inevitably follow a slip. There did seem, however, to be just a chance that a man standing on the top of the ridge at E might be able to stretch across to F (about 7 feet away), provided a second man could make a bridge with his shoulders half-way between the two points. This was the way in which we did the climb. The second man mounted half-way up the roof between the points F and E. With his right hand he was able to get a firm grip of the ridge at E, he then bent in towards the wall of the Chapel Court and supported himself with his left hand on the wall. He was now in a very firm position, although he was standing some three feet up the roof. The leader was still roped to the third man at D. In a moment he had stepped across the human bridge, and the swing over the corner of the roof into the gutter at F was a simple matter.

Throughout the ascent the climbing is comparatively easy, and it is only the pioneering of it which gave trouble. It was a great moment when we first attained the point F, and the silent cheers which we sent up were only noiseless because of the proximity of the Dean.

Chapel Court: The circuit of Chapel Court presents no difficulty, and the only object of interest is the Pinnacle, which is built on the edge of a broad leaden platform. It is quite easy to climb on to the top of the cupola. The first pitch is best done by the human-ladder method. The iron spire to which the weather-cock is attached is not very secure, and care is needed if it be desired to touch the highest point.

Descent from Chapel Court to the Col: Having completed the circuit of Chapel Court we were now faced with the problem of the descent on to the col. The first man roped down. The second man descended by the human-ladder method, using the rope when necessary. The third and last man of the party also came down by the human-ladder method, and was able to benefit by the rope which he had previously placed round the chimney stack H (see sketch, p. 20) and lowered to the second member of the party, who stood below to hold it firm.

Ascent from the Col to Dean's Highway: Having descended as far as the point C, the party can choose between two alternatives: (1) to climb down to the ground by the way they came; (2) to scale the north face of Second Court and finish on Dean's Highway. This latter alternative is made possible by a pipe, which runs up the wall for about 18 feet and stops just short of the battlements, ending in a large square bowl. The first six feet of the climb are not difficult, and one is soon able to stand on the upper moulding of a window just on the right of the pipe. Soon afterwards, however, one is held up by the fact that the pipe is too close into the wall. The highest hand-hold that one can find is just above the level of the knees, so that the knees must grip the pipe as firmly as possible, while the toes find much-needed, if insecure, support from a small staple which encircles the pipe. While still in this highly unstable position the climber must now let go of the pipe with his left hand. With a very long stretch of the arm he can just reach above the next staple, immediately below the bowl of the pipe. Here there is space enough to allow the fingers to be inserted. Without any hesitation the right hand is brought up and finds a finger grip on the ornamental rib which runs round the face of the bowl. The feet and knees still cling to the pipe as best they can, and the left hand is brought rapidly up to the lip of the bowl itself. It is now possible to draw oneself up until one can kneel on the bowl. The window-sill on the right offers a tempting resting place, but the climber should pass it by. For if he steps on to it he will find that it is very difficult to pull himself up sideways on to the bowl of the pipe. The scramble from the bowl to the battlements presents no difficulty, and the climber can now choose his own way back to his rooms.

The Chapel Court climb has an entity of its own, in that it can be climbed from the ground, and for that reason it will always exercise a fascination upon climbers. The narrow beam of light, which streams from a certain open window not thirty feet away, will add considerably to the excitement, and will also serve to prevent the climb from being overdone. For it is no light test of skill to climb in silence for three-quarters of an hour up pipes and over roofs, paying out rope and hauling it in, without dislodging the smallest of hand-holds or cracking even the loosest of slates.

Route E: New Court

The complete circuit of New Court has not yet been made, for we have never attempted to climb from the roof of the Cloisters to the roof of the main building, or vice versa. An unpleasant looking drain-pipe offers the only line of attack; the chances of success appear small, and the undertaking extremely hazardous.

Main Building: The roof of the main building can be reached from several windows. In each case the climb, though not difficult, is a pretty one. A rope should most

Great Pinnacle, New Court.

A to B: 12ft. B to C: 14ft. C to D: 12ft. D to E: 7ft.

certainly be used, as a slip would mean a fall of at least forty feet. Once on the roof, the circuit of the main building can be made in about half an hour. The climbing is uninteresting, but there is a very pretty view of the river, library, and Master's garden. Care is required, when walking in the gulleys beside the battlements, to avoid the broad drainage holes (some two feet deep) which occur at intervals of twenty yards and at almost every corner. The roofs of the two wing-blocks are rambling and broken up by cat-walls.

Great Pinnacle: The New Court range is entirely dominated by the Great Pinnacle. It is one of the highest points in St John's and second only to Chapel Tower itself. As soon as we reach the roof of New Court, all eyes are drawn irresistibly towards it. Its ascent offers the most varied climbing, and comes up to all expectations. In fact, although it is not difficult, it is probably the most thrilling climb in St John's. The final ascent is made upon such slender material that it feels almost as though the pinnacle were swaying in the wind. The climb may be divided into four pitches (see sketch, p. 30).

(1) A to B (about 12 feet). This is of the blank-wall type of climb, and is best negotiated by the human-ladder method. The man at the bottom has a firm foot-hold, as the roof upon which he stands slopes very gradually. The pitch can be climbed without assistance from below, but it is very hard.

(2) B to C (about 14 feet). This is the most interesting pitch of all. It is possible to climb up the side of the flying buttress by embracing it with arms and legs and swarming up it as though it were a small-sized tree. The ledges on the outside edge of the buttress afford a valuable grip for the legs; and the ornamentations of the inside of the arch (marked BBB in sketch) are quite invaluable for the hands. They can be reached almost at once and are firm, but the angle at which they curve makes them a little awkward. When one has climbed about eight feet up the buttress, it is possible to swing over on to the bridge, which connects the buttress with the main pinnacle. A secure resting-place is found behind the battlements at the point C.

A more difficult way of tackling the pitch is to do a back-and-knee climb between the buttress and the main pinnacle. The swing over on to the bridge at the top, which looks so difficult from below, is quite easy.

(3) C to D (about 12 feet). This is very simple, but rather thrilling, as it is ornamentation climbing all the way, and one trembles to think of what would happen if an ornament broke. Everything is firm, however. The large stone moulding at D is best surmounted by sitting astride upon it.

(4) D to E (about 7 feet). By raising oneself gradually from the sitting position and making a long stretch of the arm, the hand can be placed on top of the gilded crown which surmounts the weather-cock. By moonlight it looks very pretty!

One is scarcely tempted to remain long at the point E, and it is not until one has descended to the security of the battlements at C that one stops to admire the view and realise how magnificent it is. The remainder of the descent is made in exactly the same way as the ascent. The Pinnacle has been climbed throughout without rope, but it is highly inadvisable. Anchorages can be found at the points B and C. The former is uncomfortable, the latter first class.

The Corner Towers: The only other object of interest on the New Court heights are the four Corner Towers, which flank Great Pinnacle and stand some fifteen yards from it. They have so far withstood all attacks made upon them. By standing on someone's shoulders, you can reach a ledge which runs round the Tower about thirteen feet up. The other man can then lift you still higher with his arms, until you reach the mouldings of the windows about sixteen feet up. Unfortunately the windows are bricked or blocked up, and it is impossible to get any grip on the mouldings in spite of the fact that they are well ornamented. If a grip could only be found it should be possible to climb the remaining five or six feet.

The Cloisters: From the grass plot in New Court it is possible to climb on to the roof of the Cloisters by means of the pipes which run up the side of the buttresses. Wooden boards have been inserted between the pipe and the wall for the first twelve feet or so; but once the top of the board is reached, there is no real difficulty. The shape of the buttress helps considerably throughout the climb. The roof of the Cloisters offers nothing of interest.

Route F:
Bridge of Sighs

The combination of a good climb and pleasing sur-
roundings make this one of the most charming routes
in the College. A glance at the drawing of the Bridge of
Sighs gives some idea of the picturesque views one sees
on every hand from the roof of the bridge, especially if
one is lucky enough to do it on a perfectly calm moonlit
night. Added to which there are some tricky little bits in
the climb, with the river below – wet, but soft to fall on!

A commencement is made from the north-east corner of Third Court (see sketch, p. 16) from the ground

into Furnace Hole. This is quite a good little test of skilful climbing, but will be surmounted without much difficulty. From here it is possible to reach the river by turning to the left round a buttress. One next makes for the Bridge of Sighs by means of a sloping roof overlooking the river. This brings us to the climb proper (see sketch of Bridge of Sighs, p. 36). A drainpipe is made use of for the first ten feet. It does not continue high enough for the top of the bridge to be reached with the hand. It is therefore necessary to leave the pipe and work along a narrow ledge towards the right. On rounding a buttress the right foot can work its way up the ledge which curves round the top of the window (marked A in sketch). This brings us right over the river, and a fall would mean a ducking. The climber can now grip the top of the bridge and pull himself up.

Explorations have proved that to climb from the bridge to the top of New Court would be both difficult and dangerous. We doubt whether this climb will ever be accomplished, although we say it with all reserve.

The climb from the other end of the bridge to the top of the Third Court buildings can be made in two ways.

(1) Straight up the face of the wall by the human-ladder method. A flimsy leaden lightning-conductor on the left gives a highly insecure handhold at the critical moment, and just makes the climb possible. (2) By means of the square pipe which runs up the wall to the right of the bridge and overhangs the river. A convenient window-sill on the left of the pipe offers a standing place, from which the bowl of the pipe can be reached with the right hand. If the window is open the left hand can find an admirable grip inside. It is not hard to pull up on to the bowl, and from there to reach the battlements. A rope is, however, advisable, as a slip would mean a fall of thirty feet into a bare two feet of water.

Route G:
From St John's
to Trinity

Ivy Arch: In between Trinity Chapel and the corner of St John's there is a picturesque old archway, almost buried in ivy, which can be seen any day from the street. Thanks to this arch it is possible to climb by the roofs from St John's into Trinity, or vice versa. The point from which we start in St John's is, of course, the corner of the Essex Building nearest to St John's Street.

Climbing over the balustrade (marked A in sketch)

Ivy Arch. A to B: 7ft. Distance from B to wall: 3ft.

one finds a convenient ledge (marked X). The left knee
is kept firm upon the ledge, while the right foot 'fishes'
for the landing place (marked B). It is buried in the ivy,
but once it is found it cannot be mistaken for a bough
of the ivy. The stretch is about six feet, and the gap
between the arch and the wall of the College is about
three feet. The climb is not really difficult, but a rope
is advisable. The whole trouble lies in finding the exact

spot for the feet to land on. The ivy, which grows all over the arch, completely hides its real shape. It is not round, as one thinks, but in the shape of steps. It is far easier to climb back from the arch on to the roof.

Once the Trinity side of Ivy Arch is reached, there is no further difficulty. Follow the line of least resistance among the lower roofs which run parallel to St John's Lane. Go past the back windows of the Junior Common Room in Trinity, past the curious buttress-chimney, and you will come to a narrow little roof (about three feet wide) which slopes steeply down towards you from the higher roofs. It is not difficult to climb it, and you find yourself on a flat lead between two ridges (leading off to the left). Follow it until you can go no farther; then mount the ridge on the right and proceed along it as far as King Edward's Tower. You are now upon the roof of the Bursary. On the right is the Fellows' Bowling Green, and on the left you have the awe-inspiring walls of Trinity Chapel and its tall chimney. In front and slightly to the right is the roof of the Munro Building. This can be reached without much difficulty, and you are now at the foot of King Edward's Tower. The entire range of Trinity roofs is at your feet. Two men climbing quickly can reach this point in fifteen minutes from St John's, but care is required on top of the Bursary, as Dons have been known to call out and inquire into matters.

Appendix I:
The Best Climbs in
St John's and Trinity

Although there is little or nothing to choose between the climbing-fields of Trinity and St John's, we are inclined to think that the Bridge of Sighs and Great Pinnacle climbs are prettier and more attractive than any that are to be found in Trinity – the Bridge of Sighs, by reason of its romantic setting and the neatness of its climbing; Great Pinnacle, by reason of the slender material and the height and variety of the ascent. The pearl of all climbs, however, belongs unquestionably to Trinity, for the back-and-knee ascent up the famous Library Chimney is far and away the most exhausting and dangerous climb in either College. In this connection it is curious to note the almost complete lack of back-and-knee climbs in St John's.

For those who enjoy long-distance trips we would recommend the climb from the Garret Hostel Lane end of New Court, Trinity, to the Bridge Street end of Chapel Court, St John's. This is the farthest distance that can be accomplished in one direction, and several alternative routes are available for it.

The two following climbs may be regarded as 'Pontes Assinorum', for which only a good head is required:

- Library Traverse (Trinity),
- Library Arch (St John's).

Good balance tests are found in:

- The Dip (New Court, Trinity),
- First Pitch of Chapel Court Col. (St John's),
- Descent from Trinity Chapel on to Newton Roof.

The following make neat climbs:

- King Edward's Tower (Trinity),
- Bridge of Sighs (St John's).

Team-work and combination are shown to advantage in:

- I Court Climb (Trinity),
- Chapel Court Col. (St John's).

More difficult climbs are:

- Great Pinnacle (St John's),
- Great Gateway (Trinity),
- Main Gateway (St John's).

Most difficult of all:

- Library Chimney (Trinity).

Appendix II:
On Roof Climbing

Man is a strange kind of animal. He thinks he has reason for everything he does; but when we come to analyse his actions, we find that all of them are prompted by the mere primaeval instincts of his ancestor, the ape. The evolution shows itself in a thousand little ways, and every man to some extent 'reverts to type'. Those of us, in whose blood the primitive instincts run most freely, must needs go climbing on the roofs, while our more fortunate brothers rest content until the summer, before they give full rein to their simian propensities upon the Jungfrau or the Matterhorn.

There is a wonderful and indefinable charm about the roofs, somewhat akin to the fascination of the mountains; and the man who falls beneath the spell of either is drawn so irresistibly towards them that he must yield to the magic of their call.

Here in the lowlands of England, within the reach of all, are walls of stone as smooth as any wall of ice, and overhanging eaves as treacherous as any cornice of snow. It is hard that we may not climb until after dusk; but the moonlight lends enchantment to the scene, and throws the shadows into such black relief that a paltry drop of twenty feet appears a bottomless abyss. There are views, too, upon these roofs that go unheeded by the multitude; and it is fitting that the most picturesque of all should be the prize of those who achieve the apparently impossible and reach the summit of the Library in Trinity. What could be more lovely than the silver streak of river, which winds through the trees towards St John's, until it fades into the darkness beneath the Bridge of Sighs? Many a lover of Cambridge would walk a hundred miles to paint the scene.

Only we of the brotherhood know the joy of the cigarette that is lit as we lie full length on the leads, hands all a-tremble, every muscle tingling with the effort and excitement of the climb just accomplished. Truly, it is a noble sport and worthy of man. What pride we feel on surmounting a pitch by an insecure hand-hold, without dislodging so much as a stone from the crumbling ledge! What moments of suspense there are in a back-and-knee climb, when the body is wedged over space in the narrow gap between two walls! What thrills we find in a delicate balancing feat.

Then, when it is all over and we are gathered round the fire to sip the brew of cocoa, we talk and talk, till the hour grows late, about our climbing and the 'rhythm of the rope'; and if the conversation flags, we pass a resolution that we ask the Blues' Committee to grant us all a Blue!!